AN ORCHID ASTRONOMY

UNIVERSITY OF CALGARY
Press

AN ORCHID ASTRONOMY

TASNUVA HAYDEN

Brave & Brilliant Series
ISSN 2371-7238 (Print) ISSN 2371-7246 (Online)

University of Calgary Press
2500 University Drive NW
Calgary, Alberta
Canada T2N 1N4
press.ucalgary.ca

LIBRARY AND ARCHIVES CANADA CATALOGUING IN PUBLICATION

Title: An orchid astronomy / Tasnuva Hayden.
Names: Hayden, Tasnuva, author.
Series: Brave & brilliant series ; no. 26.
Description: Series statement: Brave & brilliant series ; no. 26
Identifiers: Canadiana (print) 20220155410 | Canadiana (ebook) 20220155461 | ISBN 9781773852713 (softcover) | ISBN 9781773852720 (PDF) | ISBN 9781773852737 (EPUB)
Subjects: LCGFT: Poetry.
Classification: LCC PS8615.A8348 O73 2022 | DDC C811/.6—dc23

The University of Calgary Press acknowledges the support of the Government of Alberta through the Alberta Media Fund for our publications. We acknowledge the financial support of the Government of Canada. We acknowledge the financial support of the Canada Council for the Arts for our publishing program.

Canada Council   Conseil des Arts
for the Arts   du Canada

Alberta
Government

Printed and bound in Canada by Marquis
♻ This book is printed on 60 lb Opaque Smooth Natural paper

Editing by Helen Hajnoczky
Cover art by Fraser Wright
Cover design, page design, and typesetting by Melina Cusano

CONTENTS

CORONA BOREALIS I

boreal

frosted

constellation

bloom

exploded

necropolis

zero

SCHOLARS AND REINDEER

Tumbling towards the centre of the galaxy, at the birth and death place of millions of stars, it's a little clot of blood that forms.

                    I no longer associate sunshine with drowning.

          The ice is melting faster and faster now.

          Every year, faster, the orchid agrees.

On the morning they found Sarvvis wrapped in kelp and seaweed, I'd caught a cold.

                              Dreams of the seascape.
                    Dulled bits of glass pressing into shoulders.
                         Spilled beer and muddy footprints.

                    At the end of spring, which came and went quickly.

Even on his deathbed, Einstein continued to explore the equations that he hoped would be candidates for a unified theory.

Roots or feet?

At the mention of Bjørn, an involuntary lump lodged in our throats.

I whispered, "the stars are out."
A bloodshot gaze simmering.

Convinced yourself that we'd be staying until the ice disappeared.

Your name starting with a diphthong.

For the second time, losing yourself inside mamma's shuttered bedroom.

Modern physics steps into the realm of mysticism.

That mamma would choose suffocation.

        Buried alive under unyielding winter
        storms.

But the Sarvvis can also cause unintended harm by becoming too curious about human life.

        A generation that has abandoned common sense—
        science and philosophy.

        A liaison. Illicitly.

The number of constellations, visible all year, increases as one moves further north.

        At your age, the word tenderness ought
        to be subjected to an inquisition.

        When facing the rhetoric of those who
        have neglected literature.

        Chaos theory as a mathematical truth.

Is that what happens when you become aware of the oblivion?

The comfort of objects. A monstrous aloe. A toy
car stuck in a pile of pebbles. A favourite tube of
lipstick. A traveller through time.

Some say Sarvvis sold his soul for Saturn's rings.

What is civilization without
literature?

From the window, watching stars.
Sand sugared across shoulders.

Hands or hooves?

Choose one of these scenarios as truth.
Can scholars negotiate with reindeer?

The familiar smell of synthetic pine.
The unbridled and the unrestrained.

You hadn't read a poem since university.

On the television screen, we watched as millions of tons of crude
spilled into the ocean, day after day.

Photographing the flora and rust.

Your eyes lingered at the neckline of my shirt.
Catalogued every mole and dimple.

That the galaxies, although vast and wide, end in some common
theme?

Entire systems of thought unravelling.

With more than a decade between us.
Squeezing out the cobwebbed remnants of summer.

Static under charcoal eyes.

How a constellation can sleep for days.

At the core, a pile of photos and no address.

Trapped in a snow globe, breathing in a pressurized
atmosphere.

Spinning on an axis of oil.

Philosophers in the apocalypse.
Protracted.

Lips that bring to mind rose-coloured
Turkish delights.

Eyelids relax, fractionally.
Slices of moonlight through lace.

Sunshine, trapped in insect wings, shimmers petroleum.

The ambulance arrived with lights and sirens flashing.
They'd taken mamma's body. Zipped her into plastic.

These are phantoms.
Imprints on vellum.
Residual feelings like pollen in the wind.

Is that all existence is? Does it provide a degree of relief?

Not knowing where the tree of life lay, buried with fossilized roots. Not acknowledged in the literature.

The scientific, or rather, the mathematical modelling of nature is quite frankly an endless task.

Did you think of me sometimes?

Virginity multiplied in driftwood.

The Upper Paleolithic was marked by a creative explosion.

An ocular occlusion accompanied by the taste of marzipan.

Her eyes bruised by grief—the colour of an oil spill. "Yes, we're unfortunate, aren't we? Dealing in such currency?"

That night mamma played her records for the last time.

You who can't pinpoint his foreignness.

The furniture draped in sheets and dust.
Infected by the curse of being neither awake nor
asleep.

"I'm hardly little anymore."

Though mamma didn't dare complete her delusion.

Of the sinking permafrost.

Before the coagulation of reindeer in traffic.
On a soggy day in June.

The orchid has a theory.

"Should I go over the parts of a flowering plant
for you?"

On the eve of the full moon, corals begin
to spawn.

Releasing streams of eggs and sperm.
Floating out to sea.

It was the reflection in the bathroom mirror which led the
scholar to question the exact timing of the transformation.

"Did you love everything about her?"
I've always wanted to ask you.

Pupils adjusting to the shade of afternoon
thunderclouds. To the torrentially-coloured
pavement. To the dusk settling inside the vehicle.

On the sea floor, surprises, as plants are not plants, but
animals that consume rotting flesh.

The record orbits to a new track.
In a space so dense it distorts gravity.

Imitation icicles, neon and sterilized.
Wrists against mahogany.

In an old legend from Varanger, a man is eventually
killed for singing songs that mocked the sun.

Taking a page from science fiction.
On the event horizon of some forgotten black hole.
Indulging in puff pastries wrapped in silver foil.
The prophecy of loneliness.

All that is impossible to know.
In a spring snow shower, a tender philosophy.

Knuckles white from clutching the telephone.

Where coral cemeteries ghost diminished
coastlines.

As da Vinci's successor, Hooke went on to make flight a matter
of public inquiry.

"If you look in the rearview, I've already left you."

To the point of obsession.
Sarvvis opens his mouth.

I find myself thinking the word murder.
More and more frequently.

Does the sky hallucinate?

For the next several months, the aurora will not
be visible.

A demoted constellation, maybe?
In the sliver where morning light spills over.
Half-man. Half-reindeer.

Can a time-bound being ever truly voyage through the cosmos?

Girl, with tiny feet.

On the wall, mamma's hungry shadow.
All the books you've yet to read.

Tears plotted on logarithmic scales.

Implying what?

Silence fills the crevice of formal space between us.

We watched the clouds from far away. You said they looked like animals, when in fact, they were graveyards.

"It's never been this warm before."

In the Newtonian sense, precession is the result of the angular velocity of rotation and the angular momentum produced by torque.

Didn't know if it was meant to be a secret or not.

The holy art often produced in the hallucinatory state.

Spent days thinking of your mouth.

Deciding all on your own that mamma's eyes were on the verge of tenderness.

Easier still, catch a petroleum wind and float away.

An orchid blooms under water.

The Boreal's on fire.

Arctic foxes pouncing in ashes.

Poised with an erratic heartbeat. Biology crept in first. As always, every moment spent together evaporated to a residual smear on our understanding of reality.

Sarvvis haloed in the morning sun.
Chipped barnacles from unknown lips.

A tooth emerges from the forehead—long as a spear.

Frame-by-frame, like a movie star, smiling, squinting, puckering, winking.

Genitals or no genitals?

Tracing for an outline of gills. For bumps in the forehead
where antlers should have been.

Waiting for you, without boundaries, an infinite black
hole.

Under the microscope of mortality,
an orchid's astronomy.

One thousand times—
I'd gladly bite back.

Checking for a pulse as the tide washes through. Which imitated,
however bleakly, the expanse of stars against the night.

The first and last time.

That which swept in from the sea.
That which swept down from the sky.

Your flaxen-haired darling.

Smiles eclipsed by rouge and spectacles.

Snow in slow motion.

The American Apollo 11 mission became the first manned space flight to land on the moon in July of 1969.

And how do you resume the life you've always led?

A double-cross of irises.
Body or soul?

Yet the theory of everything, which has been postulated since the time of Archimedes, seeks to explain physical reality through a single model.

Mamma unwrapping the pinnekjøtt.
Shuttled pearls on the counter.

One last silk stocking. Not made in China, she'd been sure to point out.

Showers until the skin withers to bone.
A measured dose.

Sarvvis below the electrical hum of ancient fluorescents.

A pinprick balanced on a house of cards.

Between the chiming of the corona, the chirping of red-throated pipits.

Who'd said that any hardship could be endured so long as it's placed within the framework of a narrative?

The aurora washing out the comet in her eyes.

In the flickering light of the television screen.

Another legend from Karasjok speaks of a man who was killed for cursing during a thunderstorm.

What is literature without civilization?

Do you remember?

You carry a constellation to church.
Under an ice blink, sing psalms.

Words map pulses of electricity on the skin.

A pair of foxes trotting on the beach or
an encyclopedia of emotions?

Long ago, the sea glass lodged in her chest had
begun to crack.

A little to the lop-side.

Then, is it safe to assume that even those equations, whatever
they may be, are in fact not unique?

A final weekend spent under the evergreens, tucked in the mountainside, drinking akevitt, talking idly. Filling each distorted minute with potato chips and dictionaries.

Measuring the passage of time where longitudes shrink.

"It's as if you're injecting a drug into your vein when you decide to join civilization."

The scholar holds onto cotton-candied fingers.

Lollipop smiles. Pistachio ice cream after the rain.

Waiting for that singular heartbeat, and knowing now, the instance of it so completely—no, it wasn't a lie.

Triton Marinus, according to the records of Gesner, was captured in Norway.

Reality being infinitely complex cannot be modelled by one symbolic structure alone.

                              The ugly parts covered in a haze.
                              Reconstituted tears pour through slits.

                    In the windowsill, gray light feathers across
                    orchid petals.

                    Blanched by the midnight sun.

            Sugar baby.
            Legs or fins?

Blood stirs until a fever latches. Even Pushkin rose to the occasion of a duel.

                    To this day, the consciousness and intelligence
                    of sea creatures have been grossly undervalued.

                    The work of a scholar is never done.

Lungs or gills?

With the early morning fog heavy at their hooves, the
reindeer stampede through carpets of bell-heather.

You'd enunciated the words—
moist, against the shell of her ear.

Insisting that you only believed in science.

A girl licks salt from parched lips.
Inhales an entire ocean off a stranger's skin.

Where to fit an illicit love when the world is on the brink of mass
extinction?

Arctic tales are stories of the sea and snow.

If not an outright lie, then at the very least,
an abomination?

We didn't trust the science then.
Consensus up for debate.

Stuck behind the voice box, full glottal stops.
At the moment of death, her personal singularity.

Fingers pressed against printed words.

It's easy to forget.

At the edge of town, the sky was dark, the Milky
Way on fire.

Asphalt glazed in the dim glow of halogen.
Do you think we imagined the right things?

Happiness pulled like a strand of silk.

Easier yet, catch a whale bone and paddle away.
Eyelashes like dorsal tufts.

Unable to fathom the mechanics of it.

White blankets and mothball linens.

His skin like blooming algae.
Trespassing on the edge of starvation.

While mamma's skin, cold ivory.
A skull decaying on the crux of a walrus graveyard.

Until the water lapped at the surface of my
dreams.

In moonlight, optically distorted, cockle and shell.
Dew collecting on urchin spines.
Watery protectors descend from the western sky.

After all this time, wondering about protocol. Whether
you and I shared a mutual understanding.

Almost forgotten, the sound of her voice.
Isbjørn cubs tumbling in puddles.

"Even this much is enough."

You suggested a hotel room.
Unbuttoning blouses in the hallway.

The star clot that slid down your leg.

Relics found nearly 40,000 years ago include symmetrical flint
tools, perforated teeth and shells, burial of the dead, scratching
on bone and antler that's intentional and ordered.

Stargazing replaced with midnight bonfires.

After a sunbath, skinny-dipping in Arctic waters.

Stiff fingers clutching the lapel of your coat. It
was midsummer before you kissed me on the
mouth.

Mamma folding origami.
Uncapping the akevitt.

Squirming in her insatiable skin—
　　　"At least you'll get to leave this shithole."

Into a landscape strewn with scrap metal, corroded pipes, crumbling concrete, where the land and the sky could never touch, could never even gallop on the same carousel.

At the age of thirty-two, not quite old enough to have a midlife crisis. But not quite young enough either.

The scientific inquiry into the ocean has been a long and fastidious endeavour.

Guilt can be rationalized within the framework of literature and civilization.

The inevitability of intelligence.
Most of the windows boarded shut.
Icebergs echoing across the galaxy.

As lipstick bleeds over icicles.

You leave her with the sensation of a scalpel
slicing open stitches, and then, subsequently, of
fingers dipping into split flesh.

"The Man in the Moone: or, A Discourse Of a Voyage thither."

In front of the mirror, in the presence of stubble and
crow's feet. A layer of fat, however thin, stretched across
your abdomen.

The fragility of flesh. That's how it will blossom.
In the middle of a beat.

I'd worn a low-cut shirt on purpose. Calculated its effect.

A queen of hearts and a queen of diamonds.

Two women share a cigarette.
This little slice of time—contained in a fish bowl.

Is it possible to grow more handsome with entropy?

The Sarvvis hauls himself back to sea.

In the low-hanging clouds, a bloated carcass smell. Gulls taking
flight at the first hint of blood on the breeze.

As though you've already made up your mind.

Speaking in a voice I'd forgotten the sound of—a pair of locked
hands glide over glossy tiles. Steam curdles over indigo skin.

Caught a stray snowflake on his snout.

I reach for an archetype.
Through the philosophy of death.

In tight pants and see-through blouses.
Nothing is said for weeks.

Catch a solar wind and fly away.

Without the existence of gravity.

A clot of blood penetrates through heavy flesh.

As a scholar, you calculate an expiration date for the Arctic.

Later, when the identity of the narwhal became known,
the European gentry reduced it to a mere false unicorn.

Tracking Bjørn's movement for years.

Blood or no blood?

The first human object to reach the surface of the moon
was the Soviet Union's Luna 2 on September 13, 1959.

How she stepped over the glacial threshold, into a room with
black windows, frosted—

"Oh, the scholar. Of course I remember."

The full moon penetrating cold water, attracting the
squid.

Marbendlar, or merfolk, appear in a plethora of cultures
worldwide.

Voiceless Sarvvis thumbs through lexicons
ripped from prehistoric tongues.

"Are you going to look him in the eye, Sophie?"

You waited in the hall with your jacket on.

In a low-lit restaurant with candles on the table, you ordered
venison, a martini with green olives.

The blood pooling on your plate.

A pleasurable mouth no less.

Wet and cold snouts under the sagging atmosphere.
Two predatory front teeth shining in the sun.

The notion of the shapeshifter has existed since prehistory.

While snow still fell on the water.

This time until the glaciers melted for good.

Since when had she aborted her thoughts?
Mamma who sat on the edge of an ice sheet.

Although the house had always been quiet,
it had never been empty.

Tightly wound into twenty-four hours.

Where ice is becoming more and more
precious?

At best, words capture a fraction of the
experience.

All of that, which could lead to the unravelling of a
carefully constructed life, measured by the rotation of
gears and planetary bodies.

Only pretending to sleep.
Detailed notes on the flesh.
On that first occasion, blinking back into time.

As if handling glass.

Eyes or no eyes?

Gold dust sprinkled across the land, however high the altitude.

He put his hand under my dress.
Gorging on schools of silver-coloured fish.

You'd cocoon her into your coat. Sometimes
when gazing at stars.

Are the seasons blurring faster and faster?

A pomegranate from the Garden of Eden or a window into the
mysteries of existence? How poetry makes man forget his
quantum nature.

Leonardo da Vinci conducted a comprehensive study of flight as recorded in the *Codice sul volo degli uccelli*, composed of cryptic notations and secret sketches in order to avoid religious objections.

Eyelids fluttered against the morning.

Forcing out a single coherent sentence.
A tightrope.

"It's actually knowledge which turns one into an addict," you explained.

How to write with blood, then as now.

Cold hardwood floors deep into November, snow whistling around the house, the heat on low, and me still in my Minnie Mouse nightshirt with no socks on.

Suffocated by steam.

In your mind, mamma had long since escaped
this soggy expanse of tundra.

As it had been in the time of Pomet, when the
existence of the sea unicorn seemed plausible.

Demanding to be brought to the edge of pain, a new study found.

Your voice crackling over the wireless—

"No, wait. Sophie? Little Sophie?"

At that time, in the shape of Arctic foxes.
When recalling love, is it recalled perfectly?

Over the crib.
Chew carefully, baby girl.

Thin veins that ran a millimetre below her pale skin. From a distance, porcelain-hard.

                              The villagers had a few theories too.
                              Blank hands without creases or life lines.

                    It was the eyes of the scholar which softened our gaze.

                    Pen in mouth. Petals on parchment.

Mapping each mortal coordinate.
The transient orbit of death.

                              Wouldn't have stopped you. No matter
                              how far.

The swell of a throat.
The line of a collar rising and falling.

                              Heaved in the light.

Into the inquiry of knowledge, they've barely begun to scratch the surface.

Words, whether on the page or in the mind, bring a degree of comfort. Lulling out a sense of security.

Often confused with entitlement.
And vice versa.

You handed me a coin. "Go pick a constellation."

Eyes closed against the froth of the sea.
Submerged as a human crucible.

Orchid blooms and antlers
offered at my feet.

CORONA BOREALIS II

instantaneous aurora beneath a nectar-saturated night
        at the threshold of a diminishing boreal canopy
        perch birds of paradise

where beaks icicle over frosted orchid centres
        caught on the breath
        —clam flesh, kelp, the name of a favourite constellation

cardiac valves bloom lunar buds
spinning 3 cm per annum from the pull of gravity

crackles magnetic fields behind marbendlar eyes
into an endless galactic haze

nimbus hallucinates crystal-shattered light
exploded in white powder at the edge of christopher's map

with each passing equinox frozen miles shrink
filter snowflakes past pendulum swings
between nebulae to the centre of a cesium atom

supernova necropolis mushroom-clouds neolithic lullabies
through ever-churning cycles of starlight

a new collection of saliva thickens in the sub-zero air

URSA MINOR I

petroleum

circumpolar

blood

clotted

broken

observation

spools

ERA OF THE MOON

Along the measured longitude of a melting landscape.

The easy beating of an adrenaline drenched heart.

As you'd guessed, almost from the beginning,
I hadn't kissed a legend before.

Light, normally travelling in straight lines, bent inside
my marble.

Her favourite milky blue.

On the top of the mossy bank, a pair of
foxes sniffed at the cold air.

Each waking hour through a shroud of
seaside fog.

"Think of that," you said, drunk off imported scotch and soda
water. "Entire systems of knowledge are being forgotten as we
speak."

Being taught the meaning of blood.
An expectation ending with your mouth.

Raisins and apples. But who can resist chocolate? Other than
eggheads like yourself—studying your dying languages?

Seduced by pure muscle.
Time ticked in an inconsistent manner.

Hadn't taken long to decide that you
were beautiful.

For the first time, I mentioned Sarvvis
out loud.

Convinced he could breathe under water.
Or even in the stratosphere.

"The map is not the territory," you reminded me.

Mamma sat with her legs crossed.

She kept a tally of temperatures.
An inventory of prehistoric methane.

Columns of light chugging back and forth.

Moving like paper kites caught on the Gulf Stream
                                        —caught a cold.

Butterflies no matter what, no matter who,
97% guaranteed.

Sarvvis with the bluest eyes, colder than
saltwater oysters.

A sixteen-year-old heart frozen and unfrozen.

For the first time, scared that summer wouldn't be long enough.

Throughout history, blood has always been the cheapest asset.

Some moments are digging into the earth for an amputated heart.

The lowest common denominator.

The ancient symbol of ouroboros, the snake eating its tail, can be found as early as 1600 BC.

A functional model for tears—
reaching infinity as it approaches infinity.

Eyelashes clump together.
Obviously. Too much TV.

Her poorly referenced map. Flattened against the table.

As black holes do not emit light, astronomers must infer their existence from the effects their gravity produces in other objects.

Rough reindeer-herder hands.
How I wanted to be touched all the time.

What kind of an answer was that?

A long-distance phone call.
A bottomless tin.

A pile of feather-light snow at the beginning of November.

You who danced with every woman in Veslefjord.

Thinner than the film on low-tide water. Because we watched.

All of us. The entire village crowding the beach.

Watched as a constellation drowned.

Removed bandages from legs, chest,
and feet.

In stars, alpha particles hit a resonance of beryllium, which in
turn hits a resonance of carbon, producing the building blocks
that give rise to life on Earth.

As mamma turned one last time, her shadow collapsed
in the tarnished light.

Nauseated by the thought of having to sit by the
punch bowl.

The shadow of a moth on his antlers.
Orchids and reindeers making small talk.

Einstein, in particular, was deeply troubled by the probabilistic
nature of quantum theory.

His albino coat as blinding as the snow.
On the death of a language.

An astronomer peers back in time.

Would you like a history lesson?

The pentagram as the identifying symbol for the cult of
Pythagoras.

Could you tell I went a little weak?

A constellation sleeps in the cracks of an ice floe.
His knees angled towards his heart-shaped chin.

Mamma had just started her doctorate at the time.

You were smoking without an ashtray.

When examined from the perspective of mathematics, from the viewpoint of infinity, the span of a human life never amounted to any time at all.

November would be suicide.
"Sophie, don't get hairspray in your eyes."

Everything that should have tasted sweet
tasted rusty.

Hips tight in their stone-washed frame.

Your throaty voice that had spoken of blood currency.
Of the reoccurring nightmares penned by civilization.
Willed into existence with the word history.

Dug my thumb to where her pulse should have been.

Orchid sepals forecasting solar highs.
Though we hadn't seen the sun for days.

Your face, so beautiful, mamma called it unnatural.

In your cubicle, craving a cigarette.

An open-ended call to slaughter.
Or a stack of open-mouthed kisses.

If you stay a little longer—

That winter when we buried her bones.

The yellow light freezes.
A heavy bouquet of musk.

Cologne, maybe?

Popping the collar of her parka.
Shielding her earlobes from the mist.

"Have you counted all the times you've been caught
praying?"

Side by side—a crown or a halo.
Or that morning when I woke up later than usual.

When you, the scholar of love, gravitated
towards Arctic circles?

Moulded valleys with your tongue.

We'd brought mayonnaise and macaroni. Cinnamon buns.
While apples thawed on the kitchen counter again.

Even when doing dishes, mamma never took off the
silver bracelets on her wrist.

In his cheeks, paper-thin capillaries,
bloodshot.

One hundred million years from now, the night sky will be
diminished of starlight.

Bringing me to the beach.
To confess what?

Polaris ripples on the ice.

Sarvvis clouds over my eyes.

Or even, thinking back, a little salty.

On the record player, Madonna belted out "Material Girl."

As seen from Earth, the neutron star appears to pulsate.

Returned to a diminished shadow on that
crumbling dial.

With a definite certainty.

The sound of his name bouncing off the rafters.

Instantaneous, of course.
The thought of pasta salad makes me gag—

Offering your scholarship before
Sarvvis beached to shore.

A fallen meteorite.

Villagers who clutch onto coincidence
as if it was destiny.

An organ from the sixties sat off to the side. Sometimes,
on Sundays, mamma would play hymns on it.

An orchid offered on the altar.

When scholars dream planets into being.

Where the exact probability can never be known.

Handsome, in spite of the gap in your teeth.
Riding the north wind.

Her fingers record perforations of light from the
centre of the galaxy.

After the sermon.
On a post-it note.

She hands me a set of coordinates.

Having been trapped on land for so long,
he's forgotten his nature.

Newton began his career as an alchemist. Seeking the mystical
union between man and the cosmos.

Returned for what should be the last time.
Lips frozen in a mile-long smile.

Our shadows taut like taffy.

Edged closer to hear about the preservation of the Sámi
languages.

A breastbone of obsidian.

In the movies, kisses look difficult to arrange.

Hinging on the importance of the observer.

Only to find not much had been written
on the languages of the ice and snow.

That your heart is a space heater.

Concealed in the smell of cinnamon and
pollen—

"Call me a little girl again."

Human knowledge is limited by both the human nervous system and the languages humans have developed.

The air, saturated with seaweed, shivered a little.

No one wanting to confess to finding the body first.

With my head on the window, counting snowflakes.

"So, you kissed him then?" Your voice like sand funnelling in my ears.

Waiting because I'm a coward at the core.
A coward in love with my human legs.

Marzipan blanketing the star charts of my dreams.

In that diminished slice of time, beyond irrelevancy.

You who hadn't shaved in weeks.

If a particle moves in extra dimensions, it has energy. For us, who can't see these extra dimensions, we think of the energy as mass.

The plot thickens when small-time villagers lurk in windows, bored of cornflakes, bored of waffles fresh out of the skillet.

Smothered in sour cream and jam.

Under the ice, impossibly. How many days spent at sea?

Lashes mummified by midwinter.

She never spoke like the rest, about weather, fish, and the night sky. Instead, she talked of Nobel Prize winners, suicide bombers, the Three Gorges Dam, floods on the plains of Bangladesh, the sins of the American government, AIDS, orgasms, the movies playing in Oslo. And what a cute smile Richard Gere has.

How to stop? Tell me how.

      The calcification of mamma's breath
      amplifying cosmic background radiations.

      Permafrost trickling through each and every cell.

            As Bjørn scavenges the beach.

            Disappearing for days at a time.
            Then pretending she came back. For me.

A glow, the colour of crushed almonds, clings to the horizon. The
cold replicating in my sinuses. Next to the body, the doctor checks
for a heartbeat through latex.

            Now, a pulse, in the shape of an almond.
            Granular between a pair of molars.

Historians look at the past and say, "I told you so."

Topped up with a whipped-cream smile.

When did he become a constellation?
He might as well have been a slab of limestone.

Maybe that's what it means to be a virgin after all. The last time
lipstick happened.

Eyes veiled by an infinite appetite for distractions.

What sorts of things can one blow up in a tin canister?

Mamma's barren lips, jagged like the
mountains rising from the sea.

Thousands of moths swarm the sky.
Maybe you laughed. Maybe you didn't.
Cradling marbles in my lap.

A crab, the size of a coin, scurried into his sea-rope hair.

On the extinction of ice.

The ancient constellations witnessing
a mass exodus of ageless spaces.

Sand siphoned into skin.

He doesn't speak our language.

A coma unfolding on empty church pews.
Gauze-wrapped fingers.

The sun smelting fog to metal.

Dreaming through a whale-song track.

Swaddled in the cocoon of mamma's hoarse
lullaby.

Inside a black hole, space and time are meaningless.

"You want some sugar with that?"
Her eyes livid. Rimmed in golden lashes.

Noses that are always getting in the way.

Some moments are crawling out of bed, shuffling for slippers,
grabbing a bucket and shovel.

It will come to a point, the orchid assures me,
when words will become senseless
unless written in blood.

How the late evening sun illuminated her face.
Soaking in the tub for hours.

Fingers shrivelled like beached jellyfish.

You tell me it begins when it begins.

At the centre of the circle of men, I see him for the first time.

Ashen lips that crackle centimetres from my own.

Some moments are for chewing down
on cardiac arrests.

While some secrets are actually common
knowledge.

The decomposition of unholy skin.
Yes, we had that discussion too.

Recognizing the futility of words.

Back and forth in four dimensions.

What were the chances of an ordinary Tuesday morning
suicide?

In the filtered light of August, she oils her arms with tanning
lotion.

Suspension bridges forming at every vector space
between our mouths.

Then, as now, the facts of life.
The laws of physics.

We'd waited for him to drown.

"A book told me so."

The face of the Sarvvis burns blue.

Storytelling that continued for days.

At a predetermined location and epoch in time.

A pinky promise.

When you smiled, I was reminded of a rabbit
badly in need of a visit to the dentist.

What had been the probability of the post-it
note?

She stepped into stilettos. Caviar and smoked
flesh as pink as my throat.

Galoshes drowned in Arctic tides.

We ate open-faced sandwiches on rye. With butter and Jarlsberg.

Everything that should have tasted rusty
tasted sweet.

She taught me how to find Polaris. Speaking of the vastness of
the universe and how someday it too would end, unravelling into
the inevitable nothingness.

Inconsistencies in every near and distant nook.
In those early days.

At the last of their tongues.

Breath condensed from our mouths.
Pencil heels catching on cobblestones.

Between countless shoulders, eyes that darted back and forth.

The way her nostrils flared when she laughed or was angry with me. Is that how mamma got seduced?

With a "you're-so-smart"?

With a pencil tracing her spinal cord?

Time, from the perspective of modern physics, leaves little room for the will of the observer.

"Don't you care about anything, Sophie?"

$$\Phi=1.6180339887\ldots$$

Footsteps cushioned in reindeer-hide boots.

Daily, as a glacier might grow.

Under ideal conditions, crystals form perfect structures
that reflect the arrangement of their atoms.

The shallow tide drags with it a seal pup with worms
for eyes.

After a cooling of hormones and the go-ahead for the
consumption of reindeer meat once more.

Catching dark matter on the tip of his tongue.

Has he kept records since the beginning of time?
Shadows slanted over bandaged eyes.

In truth, I wanted to claw at each frost-bitten vein.

In truth, tongues suckle icicled tears.

Slipping on rocks by the seashore.

White fleece drifting onto fragmented oceans.

Radiation fell from the sky.
Drizzling at leisure over Northern Europe.

You have what mamma calls calculating eyes.

On his jaws, a crescent of barnacles.

Blue wrists wrapped in seaweed. Foxes licking
ash from his face.

A tropical promise.
As a dying sun crams itself into zero space.

"Does that question have an answer? It's impossible to divide by
zero, right?"

"Not impossible. Just illogical."

And when Sarvvis disappears, the stars begin to fall.

The gossamer-thin satellite glows dimly.
At the end of the celestial hunt.

Mamma held me against her stomach.
Rose oil mixed with sweat.

Clinging to paper and ink.

Sarvvis tearing through reams and reams.

To my own embarrassment—

"Is it because we kissed?"

Coffee on your breath.
Jam trapped in sand-coloured whiskers.

Hazy cinnamon cheeks.
From the early part of October.

In free fall. Too handsome to bear.

Not sure what he means by it. Sitting where you'd sat earlier in the day.

Like a sunflower against the beige of the fridge.

What were the chances of a post-star confession?

But the orchid's dialect gives her away.

Sarvvis meets the Pleiades.

Beneath what used to be broken fingers.

Every winter, a black sky tinted with aurora and punctured with starlight filter intoxicated dreams to the Arctic—

a north wind, a white bear,
a constellation.

Staring at his wide mouth, watching as he swallows stardust.

Brows bleached supernova.

Eye colour—anonymous.
Penetrating me infrared all the while.

On the demise of a landscape.

Under the shade of the evergreens.

Tasted one hundred mouths.

In the newspaper, they publish a picture of graffiti on an
abandoned wall in Chernobyl, of children blowing soap bubbles,
though no children play in Chernobyl anymore.

Within the scope of human civilization.
He's got a biscuit tin full.

One thousand marbles across the worn floor.

Maybe, if we're lucky, we can catch a mermaid with a rose in her
hair. Whether on a spine or the sub-zero Borealis.

Young. With an unbuttoned coat.

The doctor handling the situation with gauze,
forceps, and a case of Dettol.

Open skies replaced with a claustrophobic mess
of faded wallpaper.

The day I found her post-it note.
Not knowing a thing.
The possibility of having no one.

The smell of rubbing alcohol.
A collarbone smashed to pieces.

Little girl. That's what you said.

The perfect lucidity of the insane.

That it would be a tomb.
That you keep coming back for me.

You bite off her sugared limbs first, saving the body for
last, as always.

A star clot, fetus-style, under emergency blankets.

Everyone already awake that morning was down at the beach.
Ogling. We didn't question his mortality then.

At the surge of adolescent hormones

—a dollop.

Some moments are not dreams after all.

Abandoning all grip on reality in the
Anthropocene.

Broad shoulders and calloused hands. A man of freshly pressed
clothes. As the story goes, a few weeks later, you were copulating
on the pastor's fishing boat.

Promises changed in the very moment of being.

Deriving equations in her sleep.

Under water, mapping the curvature of space.

Sarvvis slips an antler into left-behind stellar corpses.
As stars shed their exteriors between his heart and
ribcage.

"There is no culture without language," you foamed at the mouth.

Devouring freckles and maps.

A lattice in the dreamscape.

In the narrow hall, held my pulse in your throat.

The photoelectric effect was discovered in 1887.

Informing us of his mangled leg. The pulverization of the right hoof. Thirty stitches for the gash in his thigh.

White-blue hermit crabs fell on the water.

Mamma who received you with an embrace.

A chilled cloud condensed with salt.
The composition of blood.

End of winter and an unusually milky face.

Smudged on mamma's eyeshadow.

"Marbles again? Don't you want a doll, Sophie?"

All of us. Just waiting there.

A couple of starfish with broken arms.

Convinced he could will breath into existence.

Those bits of dialogue pressed dry between book covers.

The shoulder-pad era of the eighties.
Plastic garlands and bottles of hair spray.

She'd stuck the post-it on the fridge.

Radioactive marzipan in spades.

As if reminding me to make myself a sandwich
for lunch.

URSA MINOR II

orchid petals migrate petroleum
philosophies permafrosted with archetypal
currents beneath tilted solar flares to polaris
at zenith to circumpolar latitudes
where the land disintegrates to water

scrawled against eternal snow
a pint of seal's blood pinpoints coordinates
an epoch within the framework of civilization
those lazy eons submerged in caverns of ice
polaris who barely moved from year to year
an accelerated night pulse shudders
arctic starlight against clotted fox-red irises
gazes cresting north as the tide swings
in every cardinal direction
a thousand nautical miles stretched
open with broken ice and curved horizons

at the final boundaries of stellar observation
where the polar wanderer appears trapped
night after night in spools of analogue film

LYRA I

collapse

gravitation

harmonics

fractioned

post-modern

dragon

POLARIS

By counting the number of neural configurations that the human brain is able accommodate, it has been estimated that it can represent about $10^{70,000,000,000,000}$ possible thoughts.

It could be the case you were humouring me after all.

Missing the seven mountains of Bergen. The tourists clicking photos non-stop. The taste of soft ice cream in a waffle cone. Or the possibility of a toy store. Sailboats crowding the Bryggen, and on the cobblestones, multi-coloured downtown apartments. At the centre of the city park, the gazebo where we fed the ducks. Yellow buses with drivers who'd wave back at us.

How had you weaseled your way into that logical rectangle of her mind?

Stitch after stitch with slow and meticulous fingers.
The edge of his skin blunt like torn cloth.

By the sides of the tub, splashing lukewarm water onto
the floor.

Provided that the brain is not a quantum
computer.

The permanent smell of rotting seaweed.
Skin the flavour of smoke.

Within the frame of another Arctic day.
The consistency of gelatin.
Rusted salt against a tin can.

Untangled sea worms from his wispy hairs.

Flesh the colour of stewed raspberries.

At the dinner table, when you thought no one was looking, nipping on her earlobe.

Washed up from the sea, a number of little and not so little things: meteorites from ten thousand years ago, a narwhal's horn, glass beads, lumpy pearls, isbjørn claws, gilled constellations.

Strategically placed to match blood-infused cheeks.

Lips breaking into their usual smile. Never revealing any teeth.

There were rumours that summer of whales eating their young. Blue-gray skin bloated. Separated from layers of muscle.

What blood? What words?

Sarvvis sews a piece of skin.

Your nose in her freshly washed hair.

A flock of longspurs cluster outside the kitchen window.

Because it's easier to face the certainty of dreams than
the passage of time.

A stem wobbles in the wind. On the verge.

In 185 AD, Chinese astronomers recorded a guest star in
the sky—
        the first documented supernova.

In the stacks, a paper cut.

The day you brought home a potted orchid. On the back
steps, shaking rocks from your boots.

Stories that appeared out of black holes,
or was it black holes that appeared out
of stories?

I'd lie on the hardwood, crawling under the bed whenever
I thought she might wake up.

                              Asphalt hugged gangrenous hooves.

            A small packet of moonlight hovered. The metal
            breastplate held in place with bolts and nuts.

        Kicking at my raincoat from first grade. Minnie Mouse
        dancing in puddles.

                            Since the beginning of time.
                                Diluted wallpaper.
                            Can you understand it?

Seeming to know where we were going,
though no such place existed.

            The X's started out lopsided as he couldn't look
            at his chest without straining.

Bjørn lingering in a feverish part of my mind. Long before the blizzard arrived. Her steaming breath melting frost from my eyes.

Paddington propriety, don't you know?

The taste of lukewarm coffee and salami sandwiches.

In the rearview, a last glimpse of the ocean.

You left for Tromsø with a packed suitcase.
Ironed shirts and clean underwear.

She rubs her face against the collar of your shirt, striped,
worn at the elbows.

And you. You weren't above whispering in my ear.

An unclassified longing for the reindeer king.

For Bjørn trapped far north.
Forever separated from her cub.

Cherry lip gloss that sparkled in the sun.
Standing on the pier, breathing in the sea.

One thousand crystal formations mobilizing in clouds.
A season of abundant fish.

The cigarette hanging from your lip—

"Sophie, you been here before?"

The area under his fingertip fluctuated between a tickle
and a tremor.

Arms in the shape of a cross.

As Sarvvis naps in a pile of sweaters.

Ripped the plastic bag off mamma's head.

Biting hard through consonants—

Vowels shrill in the cavity of my mouth.

Fungal spores survive the conditions of interstellar space.

Her unforgettable laugh.

A bold aspiration created by boredom.
Hammered shut with pearls of blood.

Alone in mamma's kitchen.
Stirring sugar into coffee with a miniature spoon.

It's a short film. The type where the girl kicks off her
shoes. Pours fresh cream into your mouth.

In search of marooned jellyfish and sea glass.

Flaxen hair that smelled of aloe.

Gray eyes fixed on the sea and sky.
Shaving a reindeer's fur with razor and soap.

Miracles as outlined in a book.

Measures the distortion of starlight as it travels
through invisible matter.

"You must be imagining things."

"Reminds me of the discotheque."

At a time before chaos.

Orchids bathe in the tub. Steam velveting leaves and petals.

In her last October, mamma began to sleep for
sixteen hours a day.

A portable heater blasting in her face.

Even after all this time, the first snow is still beautiful, pouring
from the sky, light as Styrofoam.

                                    Naturally radioactive.
                        Of ancient bone and broken combs.

                        Moonlight evaporates off shoulders.

Wet linen hanging on the clothesline.
The scent of simulated spring.

A hot pink specimen.
Tipped water-coloured buds.

                        Arctic orchids on the hunt for the sun.
                        Seashell accumulated.

"Nothing here. Nothing here but water and stars."

Cheeks soft as over-ripe melons.
Chest hard as marble.

The day mamma brought you home.

Far too young and far too old.
Skinny-legged and thorny-fingered.

An exploration of the infinite in finite forms.

I'd never tried a cigarette before.

My breath condensed on the window.

"Want to listen to the radio?"

Starlight dripping with ink.

The skin sheared from his clavicle hung in the shape of a giant bib.

You wore a navy coat. For once knocking on the door.

Mamma always having a lick of my ice cream cone.

Sitting at the edge of the fountain.

Almonds on my throat.
Footsteps on the ceiling.

We listened to the engine hum. From time to time, looking over at me. I insisted, secrets are not written about. But you argued on that point like every other.

"It's the only thing that ever interests anyone."

Say it again. Say it one thousand times.

This property is highly reminiscent of Φ.

Slow as not to twist our ankles on the rocks.

You started the car anyway. Knowing we'd never make it back by nightfall.

Learning new words from mamma's Oxford.

Eyes glossy in the passenger window.

The smell of sea salt.
Urchins and kelp.

"Fun as a button," you said.

The twinkle in her eyes, perfect aggies.

In his book, *On Growth and Form*, Sir D'Arcy Wentworth
Thompson describes the logarithmic spiral to be a characteristic
not of the living tissues, but of the dead.

Falling madly in love with your wristwatch.

The leather strap thick and studded.

Who can say that the laws of physics have
nothing to do with it?

Once blood became commonplace.

Mamma's suicide making the evening news.

All this trouble for some books.

Next to the window, Sarvvis pours over obsolete maps.
Everything that should have tasted sweet tasted metallic.

Particles of dust channelled on a beam of light.

Been waiting for a blue sky. For a warm wind. The smell of
blooming wildflowers pressing, finally, against windowsills.
Listening to your cowboy tapes. Shifting gears. You spoke of
France. Of Neolithic cave paintings.

Using the tip of his tongue, licked the milk moustache
from his snout.

No one should have been able to survive those
temperatures.

We drove for hours without passing another car.
Without seeing another person.

Threading a needle.

Lumpy patterns on the seascape.

Wading past where the ocean meets our knees.

What else could you have wished for?

Under the melting snow.
Black. Pastel-purple. Lichen-stained.

Mamma's record player on top of the doily.
Next to the bookshelf, her armchair.

"So, you have fourteen years on me."

Kept your eyes on the road.

In a slow-moving rowboat.

Your hands between my shoulders.

She'd buy me a cone dipped in chocolate powder—

A theory of interstellar gravity.

The unification of every known force.

How many possible polygons are there with numbers of
equal straight sides that can be drawn on a two-
dimensional surface?

From under a white cotton shirt.
Bone snug against translucent skin.

Reflected sunshine.
Left out to dry after a rainstorm.
The handlebars of a bicycle in a junkyard.

Easier than a plastic bag.

In the cocoon, make a little room.

Galileo's insight about motion, most notably his assertion that
the Earth itself moves, brought upon him the wrath of the
Inquisition.

No matter how small a space may be, we can still think
of a smaller one, without ever reaching one which is
indivisible because it no longer has an extent.

The importance of coffee filters.
Hallucinating since the beginning of time.

Grabbing your arm by the sleeve—

"Look, an oystercatcher."

Spiralling for ten thousand years. A dim star in the past.

In 1975, the mathematician Benoit Mandelbrot defined fractals
as objects that do not lose their details or proportions when they
are magnified or shrunk.

Bedsheets like sails in the Arctic wind.

There, at the beginning, he battled in a downward double helix.

"Raise me from the dead, butterfly."

With a heart machine.

Mamma freezing in the middle of browning onions. Watching me drink straight from the carton.

While a rose opens its petals in the lunar
valve of my heart.

Wasted ink.
Whose blood bubbled to the surface?

Wind caught in my hair. In my lashes.

A little salt on his face. By the position of the sun, measured time.

Her voice, loud and rusted.

Notice as the number of sides gets
bigger, the figure looks more and more
like a circle.

Rolling snowballs together. One grazed her cheek.

Back when she still knew how to laugh.

Mamma's hair clogging the bathroom drain.

Your teeth that reflected her face in them.

Kissed my nose with her sunglasses on.

Over the honeycombs. Running hot water for the tub.

What sensibilities can a sixteen-year-old
really have?

Wake up. One thousand times.

Loitering for an apocalypse.
Or a flurry of socks.

Clouds that crawl away from us.

Plants aren't inclined to smile.
Only inclined for slow and sticky thoughts.

Your fingers hesitating on my zipper. "Say something."

Clots of mahogany.

A hologram of pain.

Came home with gravel-encrusted palms.
Beach splattered across my face.

My head on the ceramic tile.
The vanity fogged.

Reading books as though your life depended on it.

Devouring tins of Danish butter biscuits.

"No. You were always watching her."

Laughing at an in-your-head joke.

Over time, the hologram shrinks.

Paraffin stalactites hang from the ceiling.

Sarvvis sinks needle and thread into marrow.

Of course, it's alarming.

Of course, it seduces anyone with a
heartbeat.

Start with three sides and there is a triangle, then with four sides, then with five sides, and so it goes on forever.

Would you, given the choice, choose constellation or blood?

How strong is the undertow?

When we first scavenged him off the beach.

Whipped sand from the sheets.

Water dripping from his hair and backside.

No matter how large a space is, we can imagine a larger one, and still a larger one, and so on, without ever arriving at one which can no longer be increased.

In one of my eight-year-old hands, can't remember which, her post-it note.

Do all men taste of marzipan?

You tell me to never dog-ear a page.

By the waist, you threw her against the moss.

Where his skin bunched together. Bubbling from the
thread.

"Maybe we'll find some bird's eggs here?"

Secrets form tangent lines to parabolic curves.

Daylight flattens over the sea ice.
Intoxicated off sunlight.
Eyes streaked with Midnight Madness.

Eating tarts straight from the foil.

"Want to listen to music? How about some Tom Waits?"

"Tom who?"

Things that I swear to you—

"What's the difference between us?"

On the scholar's sofa, sleeping a deep six-year-old's sleep.
That first morning, teaching me to brew coffee.

Naïve or direct? Neither may have been the case.

A study of trees, growing over one thousand
years ago, revealed that an intense burst of
radiation had hit the Earth around 775 AD.

Moonlight cuts through dirty glass. Reflects off the metal sink,
onto a needle held between hoof and tongue.

In the silence of mamma's bedroom, the pitter-patter of eight-year-old feet. Deepest November.

There's no point in keeping track of time.

And sleeping. So much sleeping.

A male eider bobs in the water.

"Doesn't it look scared, Sophie? With those red circles around its eyes?"

Tucked the post-it into a photo frame, behind a picture of mamma and me.

Cheek-to-cheek.

A kittiwake flies towards a nesting cliff.

Mamma sipping coffee from her thermos.

Contemplating a proof.
Contemplating what else?
Reality as eleven dimensions?

Making parallel universes fashionable again?

"Men with antlers? Get a grip."

Falling asleep between the dust bunnies, a wax crayon pressed to my temple.

Eyes that never left the coastline. On one side, a pile of boulders, sharp cliffs, emerging shrubbery. Snow clumped in ditches.

He'd been floating in the water for days.
Rosy—if you buy that.

The Arctic Ocean freezes joints.
Livers and hearts.

Sarvvis in the doorway.

                              One person bites his lips.
                              And the other bleeds.

          The image of her frozen face each and every time.

                    By analyzing the photographs from the Hubble
                    Space Telescope, scientists were able to map the
                    distribution of dark matter throughout the
                    universe.

          A herd of sheep clustered in Altafjorden.
          Wailing in the water.

Lost control over boiling milk. Strands of sunlight weaving
through smoke.

                    Solar hours saturated.
                    For the funeral, folding dumplings.

Do you dream in the language of the beluga?

The last image before closing your eyes—

                    pearl lipstick on sun-chapped lips.

        Held onto Bjørn's bloated paw.

           Gray irises, soggy papier-mâché newsprint,
           crumpling under the weight of a smile.

Manx, once spoken in the Isle of Man, went extinct in 1974 with the death of its last speaker Ned Maddrell.

           After a while, the water doesn't feel so cold.
           Mamma's skin—dismembered walrus tusks.

           Covered in curtains.

Without a map, in search of treasure.

The death of 4000 languages in less than a century.

Beside her, even the water's suffocating.

For some time, brittle seashore glass, our eyes melting
from sand into marbles.

When the Turkish farmer Tevfik Esenç died in 1992, so did
Ubykh, a language from the Caucasus region that had the highest
number of consonants ever recorded.

An orchid takes root at the bottom of
the tub.

Crayola. Snapped in half.
Gold rush, an ocean of wax.

We who stood outside the door to watch
him sleep.

Φ refers to the logarithmic or equiangular spiral, the Fibonacci series extended to infinity.

You brought home a woman that wasn't her.

Black and quicksilver like jars of India ink. At the sound of my boots on the planks. The spray of the Arctic on eyelids. Sand trickling through nostrils.

A child loses her mother and Bjørn in the same day.

In the same way.

She appeared to us as a tropical flower.
As an aborted fetus.
As a cold woman lying on white sheets.

A baby narwhal's flesh.
Pristine on an iron rod.

The smoky sun evaporates. Every last ounce of blood spared. In the backyard with a pair of binoculars. Scanned the open sea. Curls pushed back from her wind-burned face.

In 1843, the southern star Eta Carinae became the second brightest star in the night sky. Outshone only by Sirius, which is almost a thousand times closer to Earth.

Fishing boats sent into the night.

Copper and bitter on the roof my mouth. Swimming towards the surf, towards the tropical waters of the south, where the albatross pecks out the eyes of starving sailors.

It could be you kiss us both at the same time.

Sunlight hours reflected on a stone dial.

I opened her mouth.
Placed the milky blue one on her tongue.

The pillow tasted of old tears.

Blew dust from mamma's star charts.
In search of a retirement home.

The orchid on the floor beside me.
Tracing for the outline of gills.
Like her, rolling marbles in my mouth.

Feeding Sarvvis a liver and cheese sandwich.

Speaking of mass extinction as though you're telling me
about your favourite TV show.

What astronomers observed in 1843 seems to have been a stellar
near-death experience. A supernova impostor.

Drowning, they say, is the most painful way to go.
Flaxen hair gathered into braids.
Her infinitely freckled cheeks.

Eyes open to creamsicle coral.

Isn't it too early for a life in crisis?

While mamma pinned her hair with bobby pins.
Stipulated that her logic was absolute.

Porch lights contouring orchid stems.
Flesh tearing through a tooth spear.

At what end?
Crossing eons of starlight.

A shoulder with a giant mole.
A single hair growing like a four-leaf clover.

Not that it can be defined as a love confession.

Rather, a reindeer-slaughterhouse
through her shirt.

The orchid's sticky voice—

"It's the only relevant parameter of any mystery
worth consuming."

Making snowballs after all.

Mamma's wide mouth slathered in magenta.

Drawn into a smile.
A pouting duckling, predatory.

If you'd bothered to come home.

The blue-green sheet of glass begins to crack. Buried in my chest.

You and I taking turns. Painting Sarvvis
onto the cereal box.

She who never really knew you.
You tell me that's what makes it easier.

Her notes strewn across the floor.

Lost socks travelling through space-time. Moving between
compressed membranes.

Flickers into existence for one millionth of a second.
Then collapses out.

Not the same cratered shoulders—
she who'll never come back.

The ice returns for one last time.
In the blink of an eye.

First recorded by the British astronomer John Herschel in 1837,
the Cat's Paw Nebula, one of the most active nurseries of massive
stars, lies near the centre of the Milky Way.

"Why do whales sound like they're crying?"

Dreaming of suspension bridges.
We made angels in the snow.

Sidereal hours stay constant because distant stars are said not to move despite the continual expansion of the universe.

Collapsed on the sofa with her face in a book.

On cushions, reconciling gravity with quantum mechanics.

Even if you stayed forever, time is running out for dictionaries and grammar books.

His cardiac arrest between my jaws.

Erased from history, though you'd argue that isn't possible.

Loud voices drifted from the drawing room.

Plastic draped over her face.

The smell of burnt almonds in snow-white air.

Reaching to tuck a red flower behind her ear.

When replicated by human hands and steel machines, it's nearly impossible to put on the same electron spin, the same subatomic whirl.

You were reading to me. Out loud. From across the moon.

Your warped reflection on the bathtub faucet.

You kissed her mole deliberately.
At the height of midsummer.

Hibernating heartbeats.

Until the ribcage rattles.
A tapered tumble of particles.

At last, tasting the mouth of the Sarvvis.

LYRA II

binary stars collapse eclipses

vibration strings discrepancy in mercury's orbit—
flawed newton's gravitation

arctic mechanics and quantum winds
codify meta-energy mathematics
dead-tissue harmonics permeate every life form—
with the exception of ginko biloba
evolved from precambrian juggernauts
four thousand million years past

a fractioned second gravitates north
coughing up scant bearings
spins the compass needle to post-modern mass extinction
narwhals logarithmic-spiral towards the ocean floor
jaws heavy with decaying flesh
above the pressure of the frozen meniscus
radiant dragon tears evaporate past vega

CASSIOPEIA I

ebony

frost-bitten

words

coral

promises

HIVE

Being young, the tears spilled exponentially.

Photographs. Always in the present tense.

With the twin LIGO detectors, a new type of astronomy
was born—

His tongue flickered. A terrifying scarlet sponge.

Holding a glass of eggnog to her lips.

Neutrinos travelling faster than light speed?

"Yes, ultimately, men seek the same things."

Mamma with a hand on her hip—

"Want to rot your teeth, Sophie?"

Prisoners of albedo.

She arrived without makeup. Dark circles sinking into her skull.
Hair piled with mismatched clips.

Dried leaves cracking under baby pink sneakers.

Steam on the bathroom ceiling.
Dew on summer grass.
Breaths in a grocery bag tallied to 200 kroner.

"For the love of god, who died?"

Attempting a game of chess.

On the horizon, the Boreal's disappearing.

We might be waiting, in this instance forever, for Bjørn to make
her summer appearance.

      In the dark, biting each other's lips.
      Whisked away by the Witch of the East.

      The bleat of a walrus pup. Background radiation
      scrambled.

                            Overhead, fighter jets.
                    A howl beating in the wind.

      At the end of the day, even if we didn't say it,
      all of Veslefjord already knew.

Tried coffee the way you liked it. In my head. Not forever.

      Digging for antlers at the centre of peeling
      flesh.

As decisive as cutting beets. Secrets tucked in biscuit tins.
In stories of mountain trolls.

Sarvvis with seashell combs.

"If you must sleep, then dream." With our backs to the window.
The sunlight keeping time across wallpaper.

An orchid's wafer-thin smile embossed in gold.

The science confirmed since before my birth.

In the archives, studying a series of satellite
images.

She won't dance for you in a dress.

At the top of the path, rock was replaced with grass and dwarf
azalea—those tiny magenta flowers in the shape of stars.

Should she have begged? Thanked you for your presence?

The glow of Christmas on her cheekbones.
A milky imprint on her lips.

In 1906, in failing health and suffering from depression,
Boltzmann committed suicide while vacationing with his wife
and daughter in Italy.

The textbook falls from the window.

Parallel train tracks only a few metres long.

In the privacy of one's room.
Margins filled with faint pencil notes.

But what right do I have to miss
the ice now?

At the beginning of his work on gravity, Newton viewed the universe as a finite system of stars and planets surrounded by an infinite empty space.

                                        Which hand?
                                        Codified in 1899.

Midnight illuminates the horizon strawberry milk. Drawing room windows suffocating with potted plants. Misted by their custodian.

              Even with constellations visiting,
              we've run out of life to live.

              Tragic until you have marbles for eyes.

         Her knuckles freshly red. Her wrists fainter than
         Jupiter's moons.

Laced with mamma's attempt at potato pancakes.

On a sloping hill, orchids predict catastrophe and magnetic storms.

Below, a secluded stretch of beach.
If the universe granted wishes.

Oblivious to my presence, you unhooked her bra.
The taste of spit, enclosed in roseroot, always foreign.

Quantum computations indicating the possibility of atomic bombs.

On top of your dresser, a pair of
pink clips on display.

The orchid speaks in a voice yearning for a cigar.

Cartwheeling over the uneven ground.

Smiling with gravel stuck between my teeth.

Flat-chested. For your pleasure.

He swam through my pupils in butterfly strokes.

Offering the king of hearts, a flush of spun yarn,
a catalogue of vanishing seabirds.

A fossil record on display.

Silt from the ocean blown into hair,
two thumbnails for lips,
a pair of black holes for eyes.

Your morning breath caught on the edge of the sheet.

Held up the bag for everyone to see—

inside, her breaths already frozen.

What will remain at the bottom of the
food chain?

His grin flickered Morse code
from across the bay.

Hobbies that include collecting stamps, drying plant specimens
between the covers of heavy books. Colour drained from where
the spine had been cracked.

"Quite frankly, Sophie, the oceans are dying."

Mamma sets up the telescope, not far
from the water's edge.

Instructions folded into the curvature of light.

Your palms on her sun-burned shoulders.
Strands of hair whistling on her neck.

Halfway through the bottle of whisky.

The fallen lip of gravity.

Dreaming, as usual, in a fountain of
holographic starlight.

Hair floated like seaweed against the tub.
Water surged against eardrums.

Catching my eye.
Then pretending you never saw me.

Crocodile-skin shoes.
Ballooning coveralls.

Mamma's beehive piled away
from her neck.

Endless because he can't wake up, or endless
because he can't sleep?

Quantum mechanics and the Arctic wind. Or was it Arctic
mechanics and the Quantum wind?

Sheets clasped to the line with cheap multi-coloured pins.
The whole box of fifty for only twenty-five kroner. Obviously
made in China.

The afternoon dulled in the hands of the clock.
The futility of petroleum jelly.
All night, watching the ceiling.

Deciphering her letters.
A telephone number. Long-distance.
Mamma, of course, had been buried long ago.

You poured yourself another drink.

Watched me from across the room.
The glass resting on your thigh.

The stability of the proton, the size of the stars, the
existence of higher elements, all appear to be finely tuned
to allow for complex life forms.

And in turn, consciousness.

Long and thin across stones—

"Did you ever think you'd be alive for this?"
Her voice muffled by wool and plastic.

When do you stop living?

Tesla had secretly developed the "Teslascope" for the
purpose of communicating with Mars.

Tracing bone and stomata.

Sunlight fluoresces through chlorophyll.
Neon-red fingertips.
The rustle of leaves on the windowsill.

All that remained were details of determining some numbers to a
greater magnitude of decimal places. To quote Lord Kelvin.

Bjørn watches me with ruptured eyes. Blood vessels
swelling like mercury.

Even through the rubber shell, my toes numb.

The thing which has changed the most, besides the unbearable chill of winter, that blasted deep freeze locking down joints, bursting water pipes, enshrouding fishing boats in frosted armour, is the omniscient presence of the sun.

But who can say?

"If you can't map the coordinates, is it just a dream?"

They said the winters were too warm.
For the ice. For the isbjørn.
For maybe the orchids too.

My period came on a day I was meant to go swimming with the girls in Alta.

The eight hundred-year-old fence, with its secret tunnels, disintegrated into ash along with the church in the fire of 1992, allegedly started by black metal enthusiasts.

On the ceiling, the absence of stars.

The north wind pushes, always, the smell of the sea inland.

I wanted to share a piece of hard caramel with you.
Some of us feel relief when someone dies.

"Light me up?"

The night we met, nibbling on burnt toast and
tomato soup.

Sat tight-lipped under a parabola. Down below, you
parked the Jeep. An unknown brunette climbing out.

Newton was a man so driven by the pursuit of truth that he once
placed a blunt needle between his eye and socket in order to
study ocular anatomy.

The beat of a heart.

Followed by three mechanical clicks.

Opening his mouth, only to remember
that no words would come out.

That's the trouble with souls.

Later, you'd sneak off to smoke your pipe by an early
morning fire.

In the tub, wishing for a possibility.
How I'd been a mermaid in a past life.

Tell me a story.
About an orchid and her flesh machine.

In 1894, physicist Albert Michelson remarked that most of the
grand unifying principles had been firmly established.

Even though it can be funny to have what you
think is secret knowledge.

Eating canned mackerel in bomb shelters.

Dousing orchids in benzene rings.

The curtains swelled into the room.
Agitated jellyfish.

"Do you miss her?" A sour taste in my mouth.

I covered mamma's face. One last time.

You tried not to laugh—

just the same, your eyes
collapsing into dark matter.

Immersed in the scent of gingerbread.
Clinked glasses together and shouted "god jul."
Never-ending brandy and candied orange peels.

Drinking your coffee, smug. "Endless? Really?"

Sticky-mouthed, I wake with his face on my shoulder.

Threw a sandal out the car window.

An error in calibration only.

Killing Archimedes was one of the biggest
Roman contributions to mathematics.

A constellation topples like bricks.
Around us, the glow of autumn.

The red supergiant Betelgeuse, seen in the constellation Orion,
can explode at any time. When that happens, it will be visible in
the daytime, outshining the Moon at night.

Determining the number of jellies I could fit into
my mouth at once—

In the dormitory, you poured me whisky.
A labyrinth of books.

How a supernova about ten light-years away
could in fact end all life on Earth.

Snow columns beneath a reindeer's hoof.
Without a doubt, caught in the rush of interstellar love.

She walked the seacoast.
Night after night, stargazing.
On the hundredth day, suffocated while sleeping.

Behind his eyes, galaxies whirlpooling.
An orchid's silhouette in the window.

Shifting my weight on the mattress—

"Were you having an affair?"

From the kitchen, mamma's laughter.

Straightened my posture for the mirror.
In every frame, hadn't I already said goodbye?

A vein comatose against a tea-coloured mole.

Feet drumming on the brass post. My spine
flattened over floorboards.

A tendency for redshifted light, confirming energy loss
due to gravity.

Would it be better if I opened my lips a little?

Unfurled flowers, tipping ultraviolet
sepals towards magnetic north.

Distended over the curvature
of a steel ribcage.

A map of the world's major languages hanging on your wall,
along with a poster of a robotic geisha.

Petals shaking in the thin sunlight—

"How could you understand her loneliness?"

That night, I lay with wet hair on your pillow.
No doubt, you had similar plans with mamma.

Facing each other, we sank into the tub.

The plastic bag wrapped around her face.

Like cowboy hands, you know?

Your knuckles, I'm especially in love with them.

With his hoof in the biscuit tin,
examining the chessboard.

She smiled, lipstick smeared across her teeth.

Mamma's papers bunched along the baseboards.

On the floor, shoulders fused together.

Sometimes, even when I want to write it. Or say it. Or think it.
I won't. Because I can't.

Work up lather by massaging a single antler at a
time.

The only thing that we can all agree on—

At the very least, he comes in the shape of a man.

At the very least, unparalleled rainforests.

A second wave of primates, perhaps?

You grabbed her by the belt.

Would gladly pay in pounds of flesh.
Filling in the blanks with whatever subconscious image.

For the first time, since he laid his eyes on me,
my breath smothered in ashes.

The chess of adoration.
We've stopped sleeping altogether.

Cheek-to-cheek kissing games.
Geological excavations.
Welcome home to dinosaurs.
A quick study of football.

        This is what the television makes me imagine.

For the weekend, floating in a snow globe.

Past the asteroid belt, switching the channel.

I dare you to call me a little girl again. Next to the
makeshift ashtray constructed from an empty egg carton.

        "I can see up your nose."
        "I can see up yours too."

Always, the smell of the sea.

Were there secrets for you?
Already photographs.

Knee-deep in reindeer manure. In ten thousand-year-old
mud, thawed.

"You ever heard of regrets, little lady?"

The Copernican principle states that there is nothing special
about Earth's place in the universe.

Learning, finally, the value of a
good compass.

After you're done seducing her, you both sit
naked in the sand.

"Bjørn? I don't think she'll be coming after all."

A celebration of ignorance.

Shadows move in beetle-steps.
When breathing is replaced with silence.

Newton's law null and void.

White blooms rotating on their own axis.

We undressed for the water.

An abandoned nursery doused in aged talcum powder.

For the funeral, they dressed me in a black dress.
Black knee socks with black shoes.

You handed me the telephone.

By the grave with my stomach tucked, my knees
bent.

Chin pointed like a compass needle.
The sunlight on my jaw.

My left leg pendulums back and forth.

His treasure cloaked in a dry seaweed collection.

Plays the orchid's knight.
Rubs crumbs from his snout.

Between sub-zero temperatures and falling snow, shook my
Lipton Yellow Label full of stamps for Borealis.

She didn't offer any stories about the stars.
Instead, she put on a Sun Ra record.
Whipped pancake batter.

Etched into Ludwig Boltzmann's tombstone in the Zentralfriedhof, near the graves of Beethoven, Brahms, Schubert, and Strauss, is a single equation, $S = k \log W$, expressing the mathematical formulation for entropy.

Punch-drunk.

Mamma—
a beautiful cadaver—
not so impossible to map after all.

The Casimir force bears witness to the fact that even the vacuum possesses energy.

Running to the nearest house
without any socks on.

Arteries pumping liquid starlight to my brain.
Driving on a road without streetlamps.

No matter where, whether it's at the kitchen table, on the
docks, in the passenger seat of your car, no matter where,
I'm tucking away this dimple, that thin scar above your
brow, October seventh's sky, a half-eaten crayon.

Orchid petals block a beam of light.

Akevitt cuts through phlegm.

In my nightgown, knocking on a scarlet door.
Snow collecting in the shaft of my boots.

As we waded uphill.

As postage floated out to sea.

When I thought you weren't looking. Only then.

Stinging of mint, with your back to me.

Absently igniting your lighter—

"I didn't know what to think."

Lullabies in forest canopies thousands of miles away.

Miracles as dominoes.

An orchid extends a leaf to collect the cloudy light.

"I should have been a great many things." Rain rolled off
her nose. "But I'm a garden by nature."

Petals close into a bud.

CASSIOPEIA II

ebony snow-queen descends her stardust throne
into jagged ice-scape frames at shallow tide
her black-hole pupils capture forever
refracted spica

phantom foxes ballet upon glass waves

solitary footprints moonbeam frost-bitten calves
devoid of condensed breaths
devoid of words inked with veins
how can it be?
only the pulse of precession remains
as exiled bjørn traverses the dark side of the moon

swimming in star-flaked waves towards curdling pockets of coral
puffing air from the same shredded seal-pup lung
earthly flesh unravelled

one thousand-year-old seashore-promises
constant as the summer solstice ice
paw prints embedded in vernal snow
sealed with a merman's kiss
an arctic orchid weaved through borealis-whipped curls

for a set of celestial virgin bones
gambled her immortal soul

CYGNUS I

star-clots

beyond

catalogued

waveforms

gods

imprisoned

viewpoint

POLAR NIGHT

A reindeer's eyes glossier than usual.
More beautiful than ever.

Hands raw from hot and soapy water.
From wringing shirtsleeves into a metal sink.

"This reality is a dump."

As a constellation ought to say.

"Would you like me to buy you a star for your
birthday?"

All of us intoxicated off the sun.
Piled the bonfire for midsummer.

Fox snouts steaming over blue-drenched cheeks.

I wrote it in blood once.
Cold like broken snow globes.

The crackle of ice.

Sweat materializing like dew.
Through clear and cold water.
Behind flower-printed curtains.

"No reason why I can't want you too."

Orchid petals sag at the height of the autumnal equinox.

In the twenty-first century, devotion is no longer so easy.
Mysteries compounding in a beehive.

Hidden inside a glacier, seeds survive nuclear fallout.

Feeling my forehead for antler stubs.

Salivating to the smell of eggs frying in butter.
From the momentary weight of macaroni
against my collarbone.

"What planet did you choose today?"

Cygnus, the northern constellation, was first catalogued by the
second century astronomer Ptolemy, and is now part of the
eighty-eight modern constellations.

That day, the grayest of eyes.

Who decides what to call it?
A kiss that bites back.

A star born from a blood clot, is that love?

To explore the galaxy, one first needs
a coordinate system—

A map. Filtered through a stopwatch.

Reindeer hide pierced open by bone.
Cylindrical tubes of flesh.
Veins and arteries curled.

Darwin's theory of evolution predicting the death of the gods
once and for all?

Which version?

Next time, it'll be better. Next time, it'll be
perfect.

Corals settling on cardiac muscle.

At midnight.
Squeezing into the bathtub.

His cheeks dimple.
Icing melting on his tongue—

To the same axis that governs the migration patterns of
polar bears. A splinter of a rose—as we wait for the end
of civilization.

Always interrupted.

Once again, Polaris has returned, blinking in the night
sky, anchoring the bearings of sailors.

And then, that faded outline, a carbon tracing on paper,
vanishes from the hilltop.

A shadow grows over the water.

"Tell me story about a merman. Or a thief." In my summer
blouse. The one with the fake pearl buttons.

Buttons that I unbutton for myself.

Clothespins in hand.

The seventy-seventh.
Picking a four-leaf clover.
The night sun baking a caramel back.

Note the times you are caught praying.
Note the weather.
The synchronicity.

A sphere of water at the nook of his neck.
At the dip of his belly button.

By now it must be clear—

you're living in an aborted version of reality.

How to explain the burden of your youth.
That insufferable gap in space-time.

Many years ago, we agreed that they were the
same thing.

A mummified child was found in a Siberian cave with beads
sewn on his leather jacket. Remnants of wildflowers on his grave.

Colours dependent on how he blinked.
On how he kept his eyelids lowered.

She was wearing lipstick again.

Tied my hair fountain-style. Mamma's plastic earrings
on my lobes—two lopsided bananas necking.

On a daily basis, sand in his shirt collar.

Collecting the waning stories of the Sámi.

He returns with corals on his skin.

The taste of blood over and over—

triple distilled.

A cloud of probability, with hours, minutes, seconds
precipitating out. Her pupils constricted. Magnified
powder-blue eyelids.

The warmth in my chest that I wanted to explain away.

An orchid spits nectar.
My mouth fills with the taste of muscle.

The biscuit tin lies buried still.

That night, pretending to not hear the bedsprings creak.

Breathing even, could be prayer.

Goosebumps like microwave popcorn.
Butterflies crammed in my stomach.

Singing the solar flares from our
throats—

"Kan du ønske mer?"

The orchid's inkpot dried with rust.

The sky like ten thousand bruises over disintegrating skin.

A freezer bag full of milk teeth.

But you kept driving. Trapped in the middle
of prehistoric darkness, an ice-age wilderness.

Library stacks that smelled of vanilla and
almonds—

the two of us shifting through alphabet
graveyards.

You were writing a book about
Sarvvis and his lost tongues.

The boundaries of the constellations were fixed
by the International Astronomical Union in 1928.

The inability to forget.
Picking at the thread on his chest.
Blood bubbled fresh at the seam.

Eclipses over his collar.

He strung pasta onto a fishing line.

With a tooth growing from my head, I dreamt
in the language of the whale.

Can we say always, so long as the magnetic field
pours from the planetary core, never gaining
weight?

Maybe they were the same thing, maybe they
were no longer the same thing, or maybe they
were almost the same.

Embers hissed on the rocks.

Between the gaps in our silhouettes—

a meteor shower.

These fluttering valves.
A game of cards.

Irises gravitating around the void of pupils.

About six thousand stars are visible with the naked eye
on a dark moonless night, though there are over 10^{13}
stars in the Milky Way galaxy alone.

At least, if he was human, it would be understandable.
But a reindeer?

Within the borders of the Arctic Circle—

five orchid petals replace star charts and maps.

No one radios for help.
In the storm, we waited for hours.
Her bedroom barred at the door.

As if channelling a winter whiteout.

It becomes the case that one spends forty nights in mourning, for such is the period required for embalming.

We were playing cops and robbers.
Hands in the air when the shirt came off.

Galoshes that arced to shore.

I could be on my knees.

In a game of chess that lasted for weeks.

At the pile of driftwood, where I pretended to look for rocks. Where he shed his fur off.

Arguments then that went on for days.

"Is that so?"

There are five types of simple orbits: radial, ballistic, stable, polar, and geosynchronous.

Joined by a fused cardiac bridge.
Fairy tales leaking through shower curtains.

We've moved with the flow of real time.
In a fake Sámi accent.
Only a glove of saliva is left behind.

Lost to a brunette with a mouthful of braces.

On the wallpaper, the phantom lights of the houses below.

"You know he doesn't speak. His heart's a machine."

Today, a bit lighter.
Not exactly blue. Not exactly green.
See-through bottle glass.

Without knowing, knees rattled together.
The music of bones. Beaches choking on ivory.

It is all dependent, science and engineering,
on frames of reference.

Brown-strapped sandals at the water's edge.
Scouring for flattened rocks.
The taste of Sarvvis in my mouth—salty and copper.

On the hilltop. In my Minnie Mouse poncho.

A cube of sugar dissolving into a finite ocean.
She fades between the raindrops.

"If you're cute, girls will save you from the brink of
extinction."

For crimes against humanity, they will try you
at The Hague—this you promised me.

You smoked while driving. For my education,
played Bitches Brew.
Licorice in the glove compartment.

In the metallic light, your irises shadowing.

A face for once, not only gray, but cheeks drenched pink. Finally.

Breath steaming between moon-chapped lips.

Wearing her crushed velvet tops.
Had mamma lived to see this day.

Around the half circumference of hips.

No exact translation.
At the boundary of language.
Maybe she'd dreamt the future after all.

"To be honest, the gods cannot comfort us. Not anymore."

All solar eclipses occur at new moon, for a duration
of up to seven minutes.

Even if I promised you once a day, it would take me 2.74 years to promise one thousand times.

The shattered sea glass wedged into the 2 mm space between my ribs and heartcage.

Rosy from the constant breeze.

Past the peak of the solstice.

"If you buy enough stars, you can build a retirement home for long after you're gone."

What do you picture when you get yourself off?
In my stomach, curdled milk.

An unpolished hoof trampling my chest. Immobilized with sweat and seawater.

A red shift. Always.

I wrote it in blood twice.

Gulls dispersing into the starlit sky.

You who can't let yourself believe
in things before they happen.

How capitalism will kill us all.

A girl-talk consultation.
Bramble over the tundra.

The teapot whistles steam until we admit to the tipping point.
A boundary condition. From which there is no return.

At the end of the hall, your wide-knuckled hands
on her bare thigh.

Placed macaroni on my neck.
Seduced young human girls.

Petals open to true north. Shuddering under
the glint of Polaris.

Yes, there are things now that I couldn't then,
write in blood.

We blew bubbles in the bathwater—

"Tell me how you've loved her."

I wouldn't have stopped you. No matter how far you wanted to
drive that night.

A foreign pulse, secret or not, until lips
are warm and wet.

Strings of saliva tumbled from my mouth.
Collecting in the cave of his throat.

A sea cucumber, on the other hand, does not taste like a
cucumber or the sea.

This year, when thirty percent of the bee population died,
the price of maize tripled. The price of rice doubled.

You become someone's heaven.

Skipping rocks on the misty water.

"Bjørn, where are you tonight? Will you come with a
snowball tucked behind your eye?"

On a piece of broken glass, the night sky shreds into
emerald and moss.

With her hair up, wearing a tight top,
she danced for you by the fire.

Dreamt into existence overnight.
Sand dunes on pillows and sheets.

Blood pinched onto plastic.

You who polished our bodies with lavender soap.

You who escaped her corpse.

Tracing me with a puffy cloud, a halo, little Mary.

A drop of toothpaste on the tip of your finger.
For when you forgot your toothbrush.

Hysterical until I vomit on your shoe.
Perched our feet on the bumper.

An imperfect simulation.

Under mamma's bed, a dehydrated mermaid
with red roses in her hair.

Everything smells of seaweed. All the time.
On the sleeve of my fraying sweater.

An oxidized kiss. There's nothing more beautiful
than a dying star.

Or the tenacity of cheap shampoo.

Our mouths open to evaporating clouds.
On the side of the dark and empty highway.

Through the authority of the Royal Astronomical
Society.

Where the rotation of the Earth causes each star and
planet to make a daily circular path around the north
celestial pole.

Even after such gallant promises to one's sixteen-year-old heart,
instantaneously that, or this, or those, disintegrated into the
quantum foam.

Would you have gladly traded in your firstborn?

Words that should have been written
with a vein.

Unlatched by marzipan.

We'd walked alone. Past the docks. Past a stretch of
broken rock. To where Bjørn had been known to roam.

"Who gave you that hickey in the shape of an eggplant?"

With the emerging world markets to save us.

"Won't you say something?"

As the sun passed through calendars.

And I wrote it again, a third or fourth time.

That night, dreaming into existence, a flower, budding
like a spiral galaxy through diffracted starlight.

Did she grow attached to the dimple in your cheek?
To her own ocular reflection in the black of your eye?

To a place that is dark, congealing with coral, swimming through
long narrow tunnels, losing our way in mirrors, puffing air from
the same shredded lung, flesh unravelling at the gap in my thigh,
wrapping around each other like weeds, as far as we can see, the
water stinging against our eyes, pearls trapped inside sea glass,
glistening in that never-ending blood hive.

Time filtered through coffee pots.

She'd taken a pair of scissors to my National Geographic.

In some versions, original sin
does not exist.

With paddle-like paws, in time to make
her spring appearance.

The villagers brought lawn chairs and beach towels.
Planted cases of beer in the water. Roasted hot dogs on
sticks. Slathered sunblock onto pale shoulders. Sharing
blankets with the girls from Alta.

Mamma's hair a multitude of flying kites.

Why was their language dying?

Warmed my hands by the vent. Each passing minute,
the horizon crimsoned. Fading to gray. Then black.

Clouds billowing on the water.

The mirror image of a minute.

Can the oscillations at the centre of an atom mean anything?

On some things we both agree.
The differences between men and gods.

Between native species and migrants.

Backlit with sunlight. What place? What time?

"Sophie slept under her body."
Slept through the morning into the night.

My hips, an ossified gyro for the location of the honey.
Could we lie in bed for eternity?

Have you ever waited for someone to drown?

While all lunar eclipses occur at full moon.

The trickle of blood
lost in the confusion of ten thousand raindrops.

Where the identity of the North Star will
gradually change over time as the celestial poles
drift through the starfield.

Hopped into the passenger seat without a second thought.
My mouth fuzzy from my first cigarette.

When our lashes touched.

But nothing so perfect as a sphere.

In this same room where I could not wake her up. All the levels
of time. From a star system to a cesium atom.
Sand in the pockets of my mouth.

Constellations grow legs. Sometimes.

We sat with our parkas on.
At a place past Polaris.

In the frosted glass, an imprint of veins.

Seagulls flocked to the beach.
Pecked at piles of kelp.

Are there some lips you want to kiss
more than others?

Alone in paradise, since the beginning of time.
Moss-coloured soap crumbled through my fingers.

Blinking flesh sea-glass green.

Not even comfort is comforting.

Tucked in warm brine.
Plucked a sea worm from the water.
Begged for a sprinkle of fertilizer.

Once there, he began to hang my clothes from the driftwood.

Cannot venture any further than this, against a wall or in
a fishing boat, and you—fornicating in the back seat of
your car, as though no one would notice.

You who'd kissed mamma on the mouth.

Unapologetic in your nudity around the house.

Stuck your head into the fridge and scowled—

"How come there's only sardines and spaghetti in here?"

Refracting like starlight through the water, they swim down to where the food is—

A splinter of glass in my heel.
Etched in panels of stained blood.
Side-by-side.

An electrochemical jolt. On the back of my calves.
Receded between the algae.

The smell of marzipan nauseating me.

His familiar bubble-gum grin.

Eyes liquefied. Glass breaking along the fault lines of bone.

Breath caught on a fishing hook.

How he'd tasted more or less
metallic in my mouth.

Two observers at different locations on the Earth's surface will
measure different altitudes and azimuths for the same star
at the same time.

At midnight, held me elevated awhile.

                The exponential decay of suffocation.

In another universe, it's all happening exactly the same,
except the two of you never made those snowballs, never
howled like foxes celebrating the vernal equinox.

On my chest, a crumpled sheet of ice—

                fractured in five parts.

Lost mothers and the slim possibility of a polar bear queen.

Everywhere they're reaching the last of their tongues.
Consistently powdered in their own pollen.

Early spring synonymous with slabs of barren ground. An aching
for wildflowers.

Your hand under my shirt.
Still to this day.

You weren't exactly a Rhodes Scholar.
We never spoke of it again.

Questioning the direction of the north wind.

When the villagers stopped rowing, only then did you
pop the umbrella.

Dipped a pen into a vein.

Eyes as plain as smudged charcoal.

On an old tram, running past streetlamps and
cobblestones in the heart of Oslo. My cheek against
mamma's arm. The fuzz of her shawl like a caterpillar in
my nostrils.

She'd bought tickets to a stiletto affair.

Aged wine and all-night dancing.

With your coat unbuttoned as usual. Dirty sea foam gauzed over
beached starfish. A dust cloud caught in my eye.

Between the two of us, the word betrayal
meant nothing.

In a child's book, maybe.

The night sky touched the earth.
Soggy star charts for the twelfth of October.
As though it was the beginning of a romance.

Moonlight on the dashboard.

His pupils dilated. Stretched into a tunnel.
Into a space hidden from the physical eye.

Swarmed by neon jellyfish.

Uncertain as he moved through a wave function.

Muted.

Since the altitude and azimuth of stars are
constantly changing, it is not possible to use a
horizontal coordinate system to catalogue their
positions.

Mamma's shawl saturated with Chanel No. 5. Deep purple
with prints of aquamarine peacocks eating red berries.

A needle slides across honeycombed tiles.

Orchids hum ancient lullabies.

Bubbles escaping towards the surface. From
where the sunlight and the moonlight and the
starlight emerged.

The orbit of my mornings.
A nimbus between our mouths.

Reindeer grazed east of the beach.

You drank straight from the bottle. It's easier than you
think. Chance meetings ending with ripped stockings.

One would like to believe the narwhal have a mysterious sound.

Pupils like black holes or black holes like pupils?
Lucid as a temptress born of a tiger.

"Has your life finally been reduced to an absurdity?"

Dusted mussel-shell blue.
My face on the shower curtain.

The sun set to horns. To the abundance of summer.

Clover in my hair. North of seventy degrees. Your thumb on my lip.

Of course, I want to hear my name out loud.

During an ordinary aurora borealis display—
pleased with a half-committed bedtime story.

In a spiralling circle, the narwhals swim around each other. Taking turns. Filling their mouths with rotting flesh.

The bubbling of the hive.

The doctor counted the seconds on his wristwatch.

We were debating the very word—

when we'd dumped the constellation's unconscious body
onto the ground.

Via mirage, a distorted sky.
Pebbles sinking on a spine.

An orchid's lip crushed to my neck. In the distance, the constant
squawking of gulls. Sand poured through the back of my shorts.

Without a doubt this time, we agreed.

Not in the least unexpected, not even by a little.
You turned to watch as the button rolled across
the carpet.

Under the pier, searching through rocks for a biscuit tin.

Had she died sometime in the night?
The reindeer that can never stand still.

Energy at the subatomic level can only be transferred in small units known as quanta. Planck's wild hypothesis.

You revved the engine—

a gaze shifting between the ice and my thighs.

The panel of sea glass cracks little by little.
The crunchy flesh of plums cools the back of my brain.

It was the first car ride you'd ever promised me.

A lock of her hair, a dog-eared page,
a favourite record.

My back on the windshield.
The natural state of things.

Can't remember her face under the sheets
anymore.

Our legs dangled over the water.

You blew smoke in my direction—

"What's that? A rib bone?"

At the utmost limits of the telescope.
Is it a clot made from a star?
The symptoms of a heart growing smaller day-by-day.

God, it's enough.

Shirts and socks in a growing pile on the floor. Joints illuminated
in the light of moth-bitten velvet.

Constellations, you said, are not creatures of
obedience.

Distant starlight filters through the atmosphere, twinkling due to a plain physical law.

On hands and knees, knowing that you won't stay forever.

∞ is the mathematical symbol for infinity. This is also the pattern in which a bee dances to communicate with the hive.

Orchids stop blooming once sunlight shrinks further and further south.

His two-part heart clicked mechanical and warm. Dreams redshifting through stellar graveyards.

"There's nothing here."

Her wrists pearled with veins.

Putting the act of murder to a vote.

Fingers clawing at my shirt.

In the copper light, a hidden hand of cards.

Ice feathers into the air. Nails curl into gravel.

Nothing so complete as the number zero.
Wanting to make her proud.

The tale of the beluga eating its newborn.
Who'd ever heard of such a thing?

Can my left lung support a baby seal under water?

In actuality, they sound like a flock of sheep.
Swimming towards that smothered light.

We spent the night sleeping in the back of your car. A bright and windy morning. You lit a cigarette on the rocks.

"En himmel full av stjerner."
"Do you have jurisdiction to buy me one?"

Veins trembled in the exposed air, twitching like dying fish out of water.

"They taste more bloody than bitter."

Space and time, although pervasive, may not be truly fundamental after all.

Sarvvis vanishes beneath the waves.

Collecting mysteries
in the shape of pearls.

"Blått hav så langt du ser."

As it always should have been.

CYGNUS II

wounded flesh star-clots theories
of every fundamental interaction
                        postulated since archimedes
                                beyond the reach of naked eyes
                                beyond un-machined hands

sailing across star nurseries
across vast physical distances
hooke telescopes occult mysteries

catalogued and pressed—
                        declination and ascension angles

on impulse radiates gamma waveforms
threaded on mathematical scaffolds

blood-hive matrices slaughter as predicted by planetary motion
                                                    the gods

on impulse tundra swans imprisoned
in godwin's bird-powered flying machine
pluck snow orchids between ursae majoris canines

on impulse approaching ice-sky singularity
from the easy viewpoint of infinity

ACKNOWLEDGEMENTS

Thank you Robert Majzels, Daniel Zomparelli, Natalie Simpson, and Tyler Hayden for spending your valuable time reading the first versions of this book, and for providing me with your sincere and honest comments.

Thank you to the team at the University of Calgary Press. It has been both an honour and a pleasure to work with such an amazing group of professionals. For the stunning cover, all credit goes to Fraser Wright for the art and Melina Cusano for the design. To my peer reviewers: though I may never know who you are, your critiques and insights helped me immensely during the editing process.

Thank you to the Calgary writing community, past and present, in particular, my friends and colleagues at *filling Station*, the professors at the University of Calgary Creative Writing Department, and the members of "The Writing Group," or "The Readers" as we are so fondly called by the staff at the Kensington Pub.

Lastly, thank you to my dear family and friends. Your support means the world to me.

Earlier versions of poems in this book have appeared in *Nōd Magazine*, *Anti-Lang*, and *Qwerty Magazine*.

Photo by Eva Gauld

TASNUVA HAYDEN is a Canadian writer of Bengali descent based in Calgary, Alberta, where she works as a consulting engineer and fiction editor for *filling Station*, Canada's experimental literary magazine. Her work has appeared in *Nōd Magazine*, *J'aipur Journal*, *Anti-Lang*, *carte blanche*, *Qwerty*, and more.

BRAVE & BRILLIANT SERIES

SERIES EDITOR:
Aritha van Herk, Professor, English, University of Calgary
ISSN 2371-7238 (PRINT) ISSN 2371-7246 (ONLINE)

Brave & Brilliant encompasses fiction, poetry, and everything in between and beyond. Bold and lively, each with its own strong and unique voice, Brave & Brilliant books entertain and engage readers with fresh and energetic approaches to storytelling and verse.